Amazing Animal Books
For Young Readers

By Rachel Smith

Mendon Cottage Books

JD-Biz Publishing

Read More Amazing Animal Books

Purchase at Amazon.com

Download Free Books!
http://MendonCottageBooks.com

Table of Contents

Introduction

Rabbits are adorable animals that many people keep as pets. They exist both in the wild and as pets in great numbers; in fact, rabbits are known for having babies, and lots of them. The reason there are so many rabbits is because they have so many babies, and with short gaps in between.

The rabbit has been shown as a trickster in many tales throughout the world; it's also considered a symbol of life and fertility, particularly in the Christian tradition. Easter is a time of year that decorations of rabbits are put up, and the rabbit is celebrated. Along with foxes, they are one of the most popular animals for folk tales.

Rabbits have long been prey animals, meaning that they are hunted by bigger predators, such as wolves or foxes. They make up for their fragile build and health by pure numbers; a lot of rabbits may not make it, but because there are so many, it doesn't make a difference. Most rabbits are not endangered.

If you want cute and cuddly, rabbits are almost the cutest pet around. They also love being petted, like a lot of domestic (tamed) animals. Rabbits make great pets.

What are rabbits?

Rabbits are members of the order Lagomorpha. This means they are all lagomorphs; there are other members of this group, including both hares and pikas. They are mammals, which means that they nurse their young.

A rabbit is not a rodent, though it is often assumed they are. Rodents are animals such as mice, rats, and capybaras. Lagomorphs were once considered rodents a couple hundred years ago, but scientists have since determined that they only have some things in common, rather than being in the same order.

Rabbits are members of the family Leporidae, along with hares. They live on every continent, except for Antarctica. There are few animals quite as widespread as the rabbit.

As a domesticated (or tamed) animal, the rabbit has been a pet for quite few years; before then, however, they were used mostly for food, or they were hunted by nobility or the rich people of the time. They were also seen as cheap food by poorer folks.

A male rabbit is called a buck, and a female rabbit is called a doe; a young rabbit is called a kitten or a kit. Rabbits can also be called bunnies; the name is usually used to refer to a younger rabbit, however.

A group of rabbits is called a warren.

What do rabbits eat?

Rabbits are herbivores. They don't eat just grass, but also weeds and other plants. They have two pairs of incisor (front) teeth, one behind the other. They use these to chop up leaves and plants.

Some rabbits eat grass, some eat brush, and some eat almost any plant. If you have a garden, you'd better beware; rabbits are likely to eat up any plants that aren't protected. They quite enjoy lettuce and other plants that humans often grow; it looks like a free buffet to them.

An albino rabbit eating.

They are grazers, and they graze usually eating almost anything for a half an hour as quickly as they can, and then eating in a pickier manner for the second half an hour. If they can, rabbits like to eat for a very long time; they will only do this if there is no threat to them, however.

Rabbits digest their foot in their intestines mostly, especially the large intestine. The food goes through the stomach and small intestines, but most of the nutrients (or the useful parts of the food) are absorbed through the large intestine. They also have a very big large intestine compared to the rest of their organs.

A diet like a rabbit's will be high in cellulose. This is something that's made in plants, and it's very hard to digest. So rabbits will sometimes eat some of their feces to get the nutrients they didn't get the first time through.

Rabbits can also eat fruits and vegetables; they have been known to enjoy raisins, bananas, and of course, carrots.

Rabbits and their appearance

Rabbits have long ears, long hind legs, and little paws. They are covered in fur, and they have huge pupils.

A lop-eared rabbit.

A rabbit can have ears that stick up, small ears (like the amami rabbit), or lop ears (meaning that they flop over and hang down). A rabbit will typically have black eyes, and a lot of the wild ones have brown fur. Their eyes are on the sides of their heads, like most prey animals.

Rabbits can come in many different colors, from black to brown to white. Some kinds of white rabbits are called albinos; they have pink or red eyes, and white fur. This type of rabbit has no pigment (color) in it.

They also have five toes on the front paws (with one dewclaw) and four toes on the back paws. Rabbits also have a little fluff of a tail; in most rabbits, it's the same color as their fur.

Rabbits have twenty-eight teeth, which is only four less than humans.

How do rabbits act?

Rabbits have many tells that will clue an owner in on what they're feeling.

For one thing, sometimes rabbits can be a little aggressive. If they are threatened, they might lung at a person or animal, or bite, or scratch. This is usually only if they are cornered, however, because a rabbit's first instinct is to run away.

A rabbit in the grass.

Rabbits also growl, and they wag their tails. This is a sign they are angry, and also possibly scared, unlike with dogs.

If a rabbit is happy, it will make squeaky noises to show this. This is only if a rabbit is really happy, not just contented; a lot of pet rabbits never make this sound.

Rabbits live in groups; most kinds, except for cottontails, live underground. They are very social creatures, meaning that they don't like to live alone.

They are crepuscular, which means that they are most awake at dawn (the rising of the sun) and dusk (the setting of the sun). A lot of them sleep with their eyes open, so that they can detect predators. They also tend to sleep around the same amount as humans.

When a rabbit spots a predator, it usually freezes, and warns the other rabbits by thumping its feet against the ground very hard. Then they run; rabbits run on their toes, and when they are not running, they tend to use their whole feet.

They also can see almost 360 degrees, meaning they can see almost all the way around their heads without turning them.

Kittens are not born ready to walk and see like, for example, horses. They are blind and hairless, and fairly helpless.

Rabbits' fur should not get wet. It can develop mold, and the experience of say, a bath, can kill a rabbit, or at least make them very sick. They are not swimming animals, and can't handle the shock.

They are very fast, and can reach high speeds, up to 30 to 40 miles per hour. That's faster than a lot of humans can go!

Rabbits will often nip to let others (rabbits and humans) know to leave them alone. This is different from defensive biting, where a rabbit bites because he or she is afraid or angry. A rabbit is mostly annoyed when they only nip.

Rabbits as pets

Rabbits make excellent pets. They are very gentle creatures, and when treated well, can be very loving pets.

A rabbit in a cage.

There are several needs for rabbits. One is to have fresh food daily; another is to have easy access to water.

Another thing for rabbits is to have space to exercise; a rabbit will be unhappy if they only have a small cage for space. Rabbits can be kept inside in a cage, so long as they are allowed exercise time, or outside in a hutch, also with a run to go into.

Rabbits enjoy being outside, and it's important to make sure they get some sunshine and fresh air. Rabbits can be taken on a leash, but they don't tend to walk along quite the same way a dog will; rabbits browse and graze instead.

Training rabbits is work that requires patience; rabbits can be trained to use a litter box, live free range in a house, and some can even learn to come when called.

Rabbits are most secure when their bottoms are supported. They get very nervous if they're held like cats or pups. A rabbit can also be picked up by the skin on their back, but care must be taken to not keep them in that position too long.

They are very easily spooked, and loud noises, sudden movements, or being cornered will startle them badly. A rabbit has a blind spot in front of its face, so it's important that they know you're reaching for them so they don't get scared. Also, their close range vision is not nearly as good as their long range vision, so it's also harder to see a human hand outstretched towards them until it's so close it frightens them.

European Rabbits

Despite the name European rabbit, this kind of rabbit lives in both southwestern Europe and northern Africa naturally; it lives in many other parts of the world as well, though it was brought there by humans and isn't native to the other parts of the world it lives in.

Two baby European rabbits.

A European rabbit will live in a warren of rabbits; they dig networks of burrows and tunnels, and all live together. This typically means less than a dozen rabbits living together.

Dung hills are used to mark rabbit territory.

These rabbits are also pretty aggressive; there will usually be one dominant male, and he will have several females. Other rabbits will have one male, one female pairs instead. They will fight each other for territory, because this type of rabbit is very territorial (meaning that they don't like strangers in their space).

A fully grown European rabbit is much better at fighting off other rabbits and some predators than a young rabbit; for this reason, mature adult rabbits will usually defend the warren.

European rabbits, like most rabbits, reproduce very rapidly. This is part of the reason they are so prevalent (widespread) in the areas they live in.

Cottontail Rabbits

Cottontail rabbits live in America, from the north to the south (except for part of South America). They are the most numerous kind of rabbit, partly because there are at least seven different kinds.

A cottontail rabbit.

Cottontail rabbits are so named because they have white tails that look a lot like cotton puffs. However, not all of them have this, and some European rabbits have this too. It's not unique to cottontails.

Instead of burrowing like their European counterparts, the cottontail rabbits make nests. They keep their young in them, fully above ground, but do their best to camouflage.

Cottontails don't sit up on their hind legs to eat; no rabbits do. Unlike squirrels and chipmunks, they simply aren't made to do it. Instead, they use their paws to turn their food while they sit on all fours and munch away.

Despite the fact the cottontail is spread all over the Americas, each kind lives in its own region without tending to leave it. There's certain kinds in South America, certain kinds in Central America, and certain kinds in different parts of North America.

The cottontail is not spread over the world the same way the European rabbit has been.

Volcano Rabbits

The volcano rabbit lives in Mexico, and is the second smallest kind of rabbit in the world. It barely weighs a pound, yet it can dig burrows 4 meters long. It lives right next to four volcanoes, though its habitat is being disturbed by humans.

Volcano rabbits are endangered, as there are only a little more than a thousand left. They are typically dark furred, and they have small ears and short legs.

They are also called teporingo or zacatuche by the Mexicans. They have been hunted by Mexicans for a very long time.

Instead of thumping the ground like other rabbits do, the volcano rabbit lets out high pitched noises to alert other rabbits of predators. They are fairly slow in open spaces, so they live in the covered area of the volcano forests.

They prefer to come out at night. They also live at a high altitude, meaning very high above sea level.

Volcano rabbits live in the area around Mexico City, so their habitat has been disturbed by things like logging and human expansion. Also, because of the change in temperature, their habitat has shrunk naturally.

Pygmy Rabbits

The pygmy rabbit is the smallest rabbit on the earth. It weighs a pound or less, and lives in North America.

It's fairly isolated compared to rabbits like the cottontail or the European. One species, the Columbia Basin Pygmy Rabbit, is listed as an endangered species by the US government; however, it is not internationally recognized as endangered.

The pygmy rabbit lives in the Western United States of America. They live mainly in areas with a lot of brush, which is good for them to hide in. It digs burrows, unlike the cottontail, and also can dig through snow if it has to.

They are solitary animals, meaning that they live alone. However, they will warn other pygmy rabbits if they see danger with high pitched noises.

Pygmy rabbits eat mainly sagebrush, unlike other rabbits that live in other areas. When they eat the sagebrush, they tend to climb very far into the bush, which is unlike most other rabbits that just nibble at the edges.

They rely heavily on thick brush to protect them from predators, such as hawks and foxes. A pygmy rabbit, like most rabbits, will make trails through the brush that it follows very closely; this makes sense because the brush can be hard to navigate otherwise.

Amami Rabbits

Amami rabbits are a rare kind of rabbit that lives in Japan on some of the islands. They have shorter ears than most rabbits.

A stamp with a picture of an Amami rabbit on it.

They also have short hind legs, bigger bodies, and smaller eyes; their fur is brown and reddish-brown.

They are nocturnal, unlike most rabbits, and they live in places such as caves during the day. The mother will dig a hole for her babies to hide in during the day and then come out at night.

Amami rabbits are endangered. They only live on two small islands in Japan near Okinawa. They are also called Ryuku rabbits, or *Amamino kuro usage* by the Japanese people.

They are the last of an ancient group of rabbits that used to live on the Asian mainland; they are like living memories of the past, long ago, when there were different creatures walking the earth.

There are only around 3000 left.

Australian Rabbits

Australian rabbits are not a breed or species of their own; in fact, there are no rabbits native to Australia. These rabbits are instead European rabbits that were brought over from England to be hunted.

The story of Australia's rabbit problem starts with a gentleman from England who decided that he wanted to hunt rabbits despite being in Australia. So he had rabbits brought over from England, and set them free on his property.

A sign against rabbit keeping in Australia.

Of course, the problem with this is that the rabbit has no natural predator in Australia, so these rabbits (along with a few that escaped from other Australians' hutches) have had so many babies that there are millions of rabbits in Australia now.

They destroy the plants for other animals who need them, and Australians have long hated the rabbit for what it does to their crops and their ecosystem.

There used to be rewards for rabbits hunted in Australia, where people would be given money for however many rabbits they caught; this was not a good method, because it barely made a dent in the rabbit population.

Another method attempted to control the rabbits (or at least keep them from spreading further throughout Australia) was to build a rabbit proof fence. This was started back in the early 1900's; however, the problem with it is that rabbits can jump very high, and they can also burrow underneath it.

For now, Australia will have to put up with rabbits.

Pikas

Pikas are a relation of the rabbit, but they are not rabbits. Their name used to be spelled pica, but they're no longer called by that name. It's also called the 'whistling hare' because of the noise it makes and its resemblance to rabbits and hares.

A

An American pika on a rock.

Pikas are less closely related to rabbits than hares. They have smaller ears, and live in colder climates, including in Europe, Asia, and North America. They live in the mountains or mountainous areas, generally very rocky terrain (land).

Pikas in Eurasia (Europe and Asia) are very social and take care of each other; they live in burrows together, and alert each other to danger.

However, in North America, pikas are very asocial, and tend to live alone. They only live with other pikas if they are mother and babies, and males and females only come together to have babies.

Pikas eat a lot of the same things most rabbits eat; this makes sense because they are in the same order, Lagomorpha. However, they are not in the same family, Leporidae.

Some pikas share their burrows with other animals, such as birds. Though, it's important to know that most pikas don't burrow quite like rabbits do; instead, they live in crevices in the rock.

Hares

Hares are in the same family as rabbits, Leporidae, and look a lot like them.

However, there are several key differences. For one thing, almost everything about a hare is longer: legs, ears, bodies. They also don't burrow, like most rabbits, but instead do the same thing as cottontails and make shallow nests.

Some types of hares, especially in North America, are known as jackrabbits; these are also not rabbits, but hares. Young hares are known as leverets, so long as they are under one year old.

Hares eat pretty much the same things as rabbits do. They are usually a bit faster.

They also have jointed skulls, which is a pretty unique thing among mammals.

They are normally shy, rather like rabbits, but during the spring they come out and start chasing and boxing each other. This is where the phrase 'mad as a march hare' comes from.

Hares are not pets, unlike rabbits; hares have never been domesticated.

A Belgian hare is not a hare; it's a rabbit that looks like a hare. It was bred that way.

Conclusion

There are many types of rabbits, and they come in many colors. Rabbits live on almost every continent. If any animal is almost worldwide, it's the rabbit.

Rabbits have been used as food, test animals, zoo animals, and pets. They have been useful to mankind in more ways than they could understand.

They are some of the cutest mammals there are, and most are thriving. The rabbit has been around for thousands upon thousands of years. They are present in our stories, and in our myths and folklore.

Some may hate the rabbit, but it is a truly interesting animal. As more studies are done, we will find out more about the rabbit's behavior and why it does what it does.

Hopefully, that day is not so far off.

Author Bio

Rachel Smith is a young author who enjoys animals. She's always wanted to get a both a guinea pig and a rabbit and have them live together. Once, she had a rabbit that was very nervous, and chewed through her leash and tried to escape. She's also had several pet mice, which were the funniest little animals to watch. She lives in Ohio with her family and writes in her spare time.

Download Free Books!
http://MendonCottageBooks.com

Purchase at Amazon.com
Website http://AmazingAnimalBooks.com

Our books are available at

1. Amazon.com

2. Barnes and Noble

3. Itunes

4. Kobo

5. Smashwords

6. Google Play Books

Download Free Books!
http://MendonCottageBooks.com

Publisher

JD-Biz Corp

P O Box 374

Mendon, Utah 84325

http://www.jd-biz.com/

Made in the USA
Middletown, DE
30 January 2020